Who Is LeBron James?

by Crystal Hubbard

illustrated by Stephen Marchesi

Penguin Workshop

Dedicated to Hank Hryniewicz, the GOAT of
Boston Herald Sports—CH

To my friends at A & D, always and forever—SM

PENGUIN WORKSHOP
An imprint of Penguin Random House LLC, New York

First published in the United States of America by Penguin Workshop,
an imprint of Penguin Random House LLC, New York, 2023

Visit us online at penguinrandomhouse.com.

Library of Congress Cataloging-in-Publication Data is available.

Printed in the United States of America

ISBN 9780593387443 (paperback)   10 9 8 7   WOR
ISBN 9780593387450 (library binding)   10 9 8 7 6 5 4 3   WOR

Contents

Who Is LeBron James?

On July 8, 2010, sports channel ESPN aired a special broadcast called *The Decision*. LeBron James was the reigning king of the National Basketball Association (NBA). King James, as he was nicknamed, was a free agent after playing for the Cleveland Cavaliers for seven seasons. Players who are free agents can choose the basketball team they wish to play for. LeBron sat down with sportscaster Jim Gray to announce the name of the basketball team he'd decided to join for the 2010–2011 season.

The Decision—as it was called—was broadcast from a Boys & Girls Club in Greenwich, Connecticut. LeBron decided to make his announcement on live TV because ESPN agreed to donate the advertising money from the broadcast's sponsors to the Boys & Girls Clubs of America organization, as well as to other charities. Throughout his career, LeBron had supported the Boys & Girls Clubs. Announcing the name of his new team on ESPN gave LeBron the chance to raise millions of dollars for the organization.

Jim Gray never asked LeBron why he agreed to have his decision televised or why it was taking place at a Boys & Girls Club. Millions of people watched the show to hear LeBron say, "In this fall . . . This is very tough. In this fall, I'm going to take my talents to South Beach and join the Miami Heat."

There were a lot of reactions to LeBron's decision. Some Cleveland Cavaliers fans felt betrayed and even burned their No. 23 jerseys! That was LeBron's jersey number. Basketball greats such as Michael Jordan and Magic Johnson criticized LeBron for making such a public display with his decision. LeBron was accused of placing his own fame above the game for announcing his decision on television. *The Decision* was the beginning of the most difficult time of LeBron's career.

Not everyone was disappointed by *The Decision*. Miami Heat fans celebrated, knowing that one of the greatest players in the game would be coming to their team. And LeBron himself knew that he was taking control of his own destiny.

CHAPTER 1
A Prince Is Born

On December 30, 1984, Gloria James gave birth to a boy at Summa Akron City Hospital in Akron, Ohio. She named him LeBron Raymone James. At sixteen years old, Gloria was a very young mother. She was determined to be a good mother. LeBron's father was not a part of his life, but LeBron had family around him. He and Gloria lived with his grandmother Freda and his uncles Curt and Terry in a house on Hickory Street. Everyone helped Gloria care for LeBron. His uncle Curt, who was only nine years old, was one of LeBron's earliest playmates. The family didn't have much money, but they had plenty of love for LeBron.

The family lived on Hickory Street in a rough

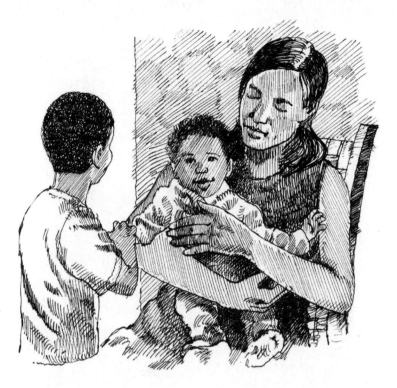

neighborhood. Under the watchful eyes and constant care of his family, especially Grandma Freda, LeBron grew into a happy, athletic little boy. The year he turned three, LeBron discovered the joy of basketball. Gloria gave him a kiddie basketball and hoop set for Christmas. Even when the hoop was raised to its highest level, little LeBron could slam-dunk the ball into the net.

That Christmas, LeBron sadly had his first experience with grief. In the early hours of Christmas morning, Grandma Freda's loving heart gave out, and she passed away. Grandma

Freda was the heart of the James family. When she died, the family had a difficult time maintaining the house on Hickory Street. It became harder to pay bills for electricity and heat. The house fell into such disrepair, it was considered unlivable. The family had to find another home.

Gloria and LeBron moved from one friend's home to another, staying as long as they could before having to go elsewhere. LeBron estimated that he and his mother moved about a dozen times between the time he was five and eight years old. All the moving meant LeBron missed a lot of school—between eighty and a hundred days in his fourth-grade year.

In 1993, LeBron began playing on a peewee football team called the East Dragons, coached by Bruce Kelker. LeBron was a shy, tall, and skinny eight-year-old when he joined the team, but he was a very good player. He scored seventeen touchdowns in his first season with the Dragons. LeBron and his mother lived with Bruce and his girlfriend for a little while. When they had to move again, Frank Walker Sr., coach of the South Side Rangers peewee football team, offered a solution.

Coach Walker recognized LeBron's athletic talent as well as the difficulties of his living situation. Without structure and stability, LeBron was at risk of joining a gang, using drugs, and

skipping school. After discussing it with his wife, Pam, Coach Walker asked Gloria if she would be willing to allow LeBron to stay with them, just until she found a more permanent place to live. The Walkers lived in a spacious home in a safe neighborhood. They had a son LeBron's age and a backyard for LeBron to play in.

Gloria had a tough decision to make. Should she allow her son to live with the Walkers and their son and two daughters? Would LeBron think she was sending him away? Would he be angry with her? Would he fit in with the Walkers and follow their rules?

The Walkers told Gloria she could visit LeBron any time she wanted. After giving it much thought, Gloria decided it would be best for LeBron to live with the Walkers while she saved enough money for a home for herself and her son.

The Walkers provided the stability and support LeBron needed. He lived with them during the week and with Gloria on weekends.

Frankie Walker Jr., Coach Walker's son, became like a brother to LeBron, although it didn't start out that way. Frankie, who had been a very good player on his father's football team, found himself competing with the big, strong, skilled LeBron. The two boys eventually became good teammates and close friends.

The Walkers made sure LeBron attended school and completed his homework. They gave him chores and other household responsibilities. LeBron had a positive male role model in Coach Walker. Pam Walker worked as an aide to US Representatives Tom Sawyer, Sherrod Brown, and Betty Sutton. She and her husband showed LeBron prominent Black people who held successful careers. He had entered a world where attending college and being successful were expected. The Walkers were exactly what Gloria and LeBron needed at that time.

Living with the Walkers gave LeBron the discipline he needed to achieve perfect attendance at Portage Path Elementary for fifth grade. He was a hardworking student and earned a B average. That was also the year LeBron began playing youth recreation league basketball at the Summit Lake Community Center. His team, the Hornets, was also coached by Frank Walker Sr.

LeBron was in sixth grade when Gloria found a nice apartment for them. One of LeBron's fondest memories of childhood was getting his key to his own home. "I knew my mom was going to be there every single day," LeBron later said. "I had my own key that I wore around my neck. Having your own key to your own crib— that's the greatest thing in the world. And you learn responsibility, because you don't dare lose that key."

CHAPTER 2
The Fab Four

It didn't take long for LeBron to become a star player for the Hornets. The power and skill he had shown playing football easily transferred to basketball. LeBron was fast. He was also graceful and had great instincts for the game. What most impressed Coach Walker was LeBron's ability to quickly learn new plays and skills. But right-handed LeBron had to work hard to learn to dribble and shoot with his left hand. In time, his left-handed layup became just as good as his right.

LeBron heeded the advice of all of his coaches. Dru Joyce II coached LeBron's Amateur Athletic Union (AAU) team, the Shooting Stars. Twelve-year-old LeBron was almost six feet tall, and he was an aggressive player who loved shooting.

Coach Joyce taught LeBron the importance of passing the ball and that great basketball players work to make their teammates stronger, too. Coach Joyce never had to repeat that lesson. LeBron began passing the ball as much as shooting it.

LeBron became best friends with a few of his Shooting Stars teammates: Dru Joyce III ("Little Dru"), Willie McGee, and Sian Cotton. The boys called themselves the Fab Four, which had first been the nickname of the superstar British rock group the Beatles.

Little Dru, the son of the coach, always spoke his mind and had the steady support of his father. Willie, the quietest of the group, was from Chicago. His parents had sent him to Akron to live with his older brother. Sian wasn't a great shooter, but he protected his teammates and grabbed lots of rebounds. Sian was a big kid who also played football.

Dru Joyce III   Willie McGee   Sian Cotton

In the summer before eighth grade, the team qualified for a national championship tournament. They didn't win, but the loss united them. They promised to work harder, stay together, and go on to win a national title.

The boys did just that. In the Fab Four's five years playing in the AAU, the Shooting Stars won six national championship titles and more than two hundred games! LeBron was such a good player, he received a lot of national attention. He was known throughout the United States as one of the best young basketball players in the nation.

When the time came for LeBron to go to high school, the expectation was that he would attend John R. Buchtel High School, a predominantly Black school in Akron with a very successful basketball program.

The Fab Four knew that Little Dru was probably too short to make Buchtel's basketball team. LeBron had to make a very important decision—whether to attend Buchtel and play for a strong team or to go elsewhere to keep the Fab Four together. The boys decided to stay together, and in 1999, they began attending St. Vincent–St. Mary High School. LeBron was fourteen years old.

Known as "St. V," the small Catholic school was strong academically. But it wasn't known as a strong basketball school. St. V's basketball coach, Keith Dambrot, was well-known to the Fab Four. Coach Dambrot instructed basketball clinics on Sundays at the local Jewish Community

St. Vincent–St. Mary High School

Center. LeBron and some of his Shooting Stars teammates had attended those clinics every week when they were in eighth grade. Coach Dambrot had assured Little Dru that at St. V, he'd get the chance to be on the basketball team and play.

Romeo Travis

Little Dru's decision to attend St. V brought the rest of the Fab Four with him. Once there, Dru, Willie, Sian, and LeBron met Romeo Travis. Romeo had an aggressive attitude, but he seemed to mellow once he became friends with the Fab Four. The boys welcomed Romeo into their friendship bubble, creating the Fab Five.

CHAPTER 3
A New World

Attending St. V was a huge culture shock for LeBron. He had never spent much time around white people, and St. V was a mostly white school. There were people who disapproved of LeBron and his friends for choosing a "white" school over Buchtel.

But basketball made LeBron feel right at home.

In his freshman year, LeBron and the rest of the Fab Five led the St. V Irish to the Ohio state high-school championship title. St. V repeated their victory in LeBron's sophomore year. The team went 26–1. LeBron averaged 25.2 points per game. He became the first sophomore to earn Ohio's Mr. Basketball award and the first to be named to *USA Today*'s All-USA team.

LeBron was seventeen years old when he saw sixteen-year-old Savannah Brinson cheerleading for Buchtel at a football game. He introduced himself to the athletic young lady with the radiant smile. He invited her to one of his basketball games, and she agreed to come watch him play.

Like so many other people in Akron, Savannah had heard of LeBron. Once she saw him play basketball, she realized that he was a superstar.

But he was also very friendly and humble. He was kind and even a little shy. LeBron invited Savannah on a date, and he took her to dinner at Outback Steakhouse. From that moment on,

Savannah was the only girl for LeBron. She said she knew LeBron really liked her because when she forgot the leftovers from dinner in his car, he drove them back to her home to give himself another chance to see her.

In the summer of 2000, six-foot-four, 170-pound LeBron attended a Five-Star Basketball camp at Robert Morris University in Pittsburgh, Pennsylvania. Many famous NBA stars had attended the camp in their younger years. Five-Star players were divided into two leagues by age, but LeBron was so much more advanced than other players his age, he was bumped up to the league for older players. LeBron didn't want to leave his teammates, so he got permission to play in *both* leagues! LeBron played four games every day rather than two. He also earned his way into the all-star games for each league. No one had ever before played in both leagues!

LeBron's junior year brought even more attention. St. V's gym wasn't big enough to hold all the people who wanted to see LeBron play! Some of those people were scouts (professionals hired to evaluate young players) and some were NBA stars. Los Angeles Lakers superstar

Shaquille O'Neal came to Akron to watch LeBron play. St. V moved some of their home games to the University of Akron, where more people could attend each game.

Five-Star Basketball Camps

The Five-Star Basketball camp was created in 1966 by Howard Garfinkel and Will Klein. The two men developed Five-Star because they loved basketball and wanted to provide a place for young players to improve their skills. Originally based in Honesdale, Pennsylvania, Five-Star spread out to

hold camps in Pittsburgh, New York, and Virginia. Between 1966 and 2008, Five-Star coached more than 250,000 players, some of whom (Michael Jordan, Patrick Ewing, Grant Hill, LeBron James, Steph Curry, Chris Bosh, Paul Pierce, Lauren Jackson, Yolanda Griffith, and many more) went on to stellar careers in the NBA and the Women's National Basketball Association (WNBA).

Sports Illustrated magazine pictured LeBron on the cover of its February 18, 2002, issue. The magazine labeled him "The Chosen One" because it hoped LeBron would become the NBA's next glowing superstar following Michael Jordan's retirement in 2003. The magazine also fueled rumors that LeBron would enter the NBA draft as a high-school junior. At six-foot-seven and 225 pounds, LeBron already had the size to compete in the NBA. He seemed to have the skill as well.

But LeBron quickly hushed rumors of entering the NBA draft. He valued getting his diploma and finishing his high-school career with the Fab Five over skipping his senior year to play in the NBA.

Michael Jordan (1963–)

Michael Jeffrey Jordan was born in Brooklyn, New York. He played college basketball for the North Carolina Tar Heels, signing with the NBA in 1984. He played for the Chicago Bulls and then the Washington Wizards. Michael retired from the Bulls twice, once in 1994 and again in 1999. Twice Michael led the Bulls to a "three-peat"—three consecutive NBA championships—for a total of six with the team.

After retiring from the Bulls in 1999, Michael joined the Wizards as part owner. He played for the team from 2001 to 2003 before retiring from the game for good. Also known by his initials, "M.J.," he is cited as basketball's GOAT—the greatest of all time.

As a player, Michael was sometimes criticized for not using his fame to bring attention to causes that affected his fans and African Americans. But in 2020, he pledged $100 million to organizations, including Black Votes Matter, which fights voter suppression in America.

CHAPTER 4
A Senior Almost Sidelined

LeBron had a senior year unlike that of any other high-school student. College basketball scouts were at his games. Companies lined up to

ask him to sign deals to represent their products as soon as he began playing professionally. The eyes of the world seemed to be on him as he tried to focus on his schoolwork, dating Savannah, and basketball games.

LeBron had to be very careful about the attention he received and how he behaved. Very specific rules govern student athletes who are being looked at by the NBA. They are not allowed to take money or valuable gifts. Breaking the rules could result in serious consequences.

The Cleveland Cavaliers (also known as "the Cavs") invited LeBron to work out with the team in spring 2002. LeBron politely turned down the invitation. NBA teams are forbidden to have contact with amateur players until they are eligible to play professionally. John Lucas,

Cleveland's coach, was suspended for the first two games of the 2002–2003 season for making the offer, and the Cavaliers had to pay a $150,000 fine because of the invitation.

LeBron's stellar high-school basketball career almost came to a shattering end because of two gifts. Gloria gave LeBron a car for his eighteenth birthday. It wasn't just any car: It was a customized GMC Hummer H2 worth $80,000.

Suspicions rose as to how the family could have afforded such an expensive vehicle. Some people assumed that LeBron must have accepted

the car, or the money to buy it, from a company that wanted LeBron to endorse its products.

Such accusations directly threatened LeBron's amateur athlete status. He wouldn't have been able to play for St. V any longer if the rumors were true. Gloria shut down the rumors by showing everyone the paperwork for the bank loan she had acquired to purchase the car. But no sooner had that problem been settled when another sprang up to again threaten LeBron's high-school playing career.

A clothing-store owner gave LeBron some

vintage sports jerseys in exchange for autographed photos. The jerseys were valued at almost $900. Such an expensive gift was considered payment for LeBron's autographs, and he was declared ineligible to play basketball. He was crushed at the thought of being unable to play the last few weeks of his senior year.

Gloria hired a lawyer to fight the decision, and it was overturned. When LeBron returned to the team, he was stronger and better than ever. He scored his personal best—fifty-two points!—in his first game back on the team. LeBron and the Fab Five pushed St. V to the finals for a fourth year in a row. They won the state championship and *USA Today* ranked them number one of all the high-school basketball teams in the United States.

By the time he graduated from St. V, LeBron had been named Mr. Ohio Basketball, Mr. Basketball, Gatorade Player of the Year, and a McDonald's All-American MVP.

CHAPTER 5
From Prep to Pro

Not many high-school basketball players go straight to the NBA following their graduations. Most players go on to play in college, where they sharpen their skills and build their size and strength to prepare for NBA careers. Kobe Bryant, Kevin Garnett, Amar'e Stoudemire, Tracy McGrady, Dwight Howard, and Moses Malone are several NBA success stories of players who went "prep to pro"— straight to the NBA from high school.

LeBron joined their ranks when he decided to skip college and enter the

NBA draft. He had the size to compete with NBA players, and he certainly had the skills. Nike was so sure of LeBron's future NBA success, the athletic company signed LeBron to a $90 million contract almost as soon as he graduated high school! When LeBron arrived at New York City's

Madison Square Garden for the 2003 NBA Draft on June 26, he was a multimillionaire before even setting foot on an NBA court. In high school LeBron had been called "King James" because of his skills and talent; now he was living up to the name by being as wealthy as a king.

LeBron, the recent high-school graduate, was clearly the top choice in the draft. His hometown team, the Cleveland Cavaliers (Cleveland is less than forty miles from Akron), won the first pick in the draft. Of course, Cleveland chose LeBron! At the time, the Cavs were tied with the Denver Nuggets for the worst record in the NBA.

Cleveland hoped LeBron, their powerful new forward, would lead the Cavaliers to greatness.

Greatness, however, takes time. There was a lot of pressure on eighteen-year-old LeBron. As long as his mother, his friends, and Savannah were in his corner, LeBron was certain there was nothing he couldn't do. He played well in his first year with the Cavaliers. LeBron averaged 20.9 points per game in his first season. At nineteen years old, he became the youngest player ever to earn Rookie of the Year honors.

In his first year with the Cavaliers, LeBron also created the LeBron James Family Foundation. The foundation helps single-parent families. LeBron never forgot how hard it had been for his mother to raise him alone. In creating the foundation,

LeBron wanted to make sure other parents had someplace to go for help when they needed it.

LeBron missed a few preseason practices before his second year with the Cavaliers. He wanted to be with Savannah on October 6, 2004, when she gave birth to their first child.

They named him LeBron Raymone James Jr. But they called him "Bronny."

Having grown up without a father, LeBron

resolved to be the very best dad he could be. Starting from the moment of Bronny's birth, LeBron would always be there for his child.

In his second season, LeBron scored an average of 27.2 points per game. He was voted into the All-Star Game for the first time. The Cavs finished the season 42–40.

In 2005, he became the youngest player at the time to score more than fifty points in a game.

East Team from the 2005 NBA All-Star Game

The next season, LeBron became the youngest player to ever win the All-Star Game MVP award. He also made his first appearance in the playoffs. The Cavs lost to the Detroit Pistons in the semifinals, but LeBron was praised for his play.

NBA All-Stars

Every year, the NBA hosts an exhibition known as the All-Star Game. The two All-Star teams are made up of the league's twenty-four most popular players. The All-Star Game is the showcase in the three-day All-Star Weekend. The first All-Star Game was played on March 2, 1951, at the famed Boston Garden. The Eastern Conference team won, 111–94.

Basketball fans, players, and the media vote to choose the five-man starting lineups for each team. The league's head coaches select the seven reserves needed to make a twelve-man lineup for each team. Coaches can't vote for players on their own teams. As of 2018, the players receiving the most votes get to be the team captains. The captains chose from the All-Star reserves to form their teams. Each team gets to play for a charity of their choosing to help make the game as competitive as possible.

LeBron helped propel Cleveland into the NBA Finals in 2007. The Cavaliers beat the Pistons to meet the San Antonio Spurs for the league championship. Unfortunately, the Spurs beat the Cavs in four games. The championship ring remained out of LeBron's grasp, but he got something else he wanted. On June 4, Savannah had another son. They named him Bryce Maximus James. Bryce's middle name is the same as that of the lead character in *Gladiator*, LeBron's favorite film.

Bryce Maximus James

LeBron spent seven seasons playing for the Cavaliers. He always played his hardest. He led Cleveland to the playoffs five times. He won the NBA scoring title by averaging thirty points per game in the 2007–2008 season.

In July 2010, LeBron James became an unrestricted free agent. Many teams wanted him to play for them. The nickname "King James" began to reflect LeBron's importance rather than just his wealth.

CHAPTER 6
The Decision and the Heat

Becoming a free agent means that a basketball player can sign with any team they want to. The New York Knicks, the Chicago Bulls, the New  Jersey Nets, the Los Angeles Clippers, and the Miami Heat all wanted LeBron to play for them. The Cavaliers, perhaps most of all, wanted LeBron to sign with them and stay in Ohio.

Sports channel ESPN wanted to televise LeBron's choice in a special broadcast they called *The Decision*. Such an event would earn lots of money from advertisers. LeBron agreed to televise his announcement only if ESPN donated that money to charity, including one of his favorite causes, the Boys & Girls Clubs of America.

LeBron sat down with sports reporter Jim Gray at a Boys & Girls Club in Connecticut to tell the nation which team he would play for in the 2010–2011 season. The decision was very difficult for him. LeBron didn't want to leave his hometown or the team that he'd been with

Jim Gray

for seven years. But he had a dream of his own. He wanted to win a championship ring.

LeBron announced that he would sign with the Miami Heat. Basketball fans in Miami were thrilled, but Cleveland fans were deeply disappointed and angry. Some fans burned their LeBron James Cavaliers jerseys. Dan Gilbert, owner of the Cavaliers, wrote an angry letter that was published in the newspaper and on the Cavaliers website. He called LeBron heartless and disloyal to the area he grew up in. He boldly declared the Cavs would

Dan Gilbert

win an NBA championship before LeBron's new team would. Basketball superstars Michael Jordan and Shaquille O'Neal also criticized LeBron for leaving the Cavs.

Jim Gray asked LeBron lots of questions, but he never asked one that might have spared LeBron such negative backlash for revealing his decision on television. He never asked LeBron why the decision was being announced at a Boys & Girls Club. And he never asked about the charitable donation LeBron had asked ESPN to make.

Fans didn't understand that LeBron was on television to raise millions of dollars for charity.

For the second time in his basketball career, LeBron faced anger and resentment from basketball fans and fellow players. Many people expressed their disapproval when LeBron and his teammates chose to play high-school basketball for St. V rather than Buchtel. The backlash hurt this time, just as it did then, but LeBron was determined to follow his dream.

LeBron joined Dwyane Wade, who was already with the Heat, and Chris Bosh, who went to the Heat when LeBron did. Together, they formed a scoring superpower. The three friends wanted to play together to increase their chances of winning a championship. It was rare for basketball players to openly take control of their team's destiny. But LeBron had done this before, when he'd chosen his high school. Back then, loyalty to a friend drove him to St. V, where the Fab Five was born.

As a professional basketball player, loyalty to his dream of a championship drove him to choose the Miami Heat, where LeBron, Dwyane, and Chris became known as "the Big Three" and "the Heatles." LeBron said that, like the Beatles, the Heatles "sell out arenas wherever they go."

The Big Three and the Miami Heat were criticized in their first season together. Although Miami basketball fans adored the Big Three, fans in rival cities resented the powerhouse LeBron, Dwyane, and Chris had created. LeBron wasn't used to being so widely disliked. The negativity weighed him down. His mood on court changed. He seemed more intense and aggressive. On December 2, 2010, he played his first game against the Cavaliers since his departure in Cleveland. LeBron was booed by the very same fans who had once cheered him.

While some hometown fans might have been upset with him, only one person's feelings mattered most to LeBron. On New Year's Eve 2011, he proposed to Savannah in Miami. And she said yes!

Team USA's Youngest Basketball Olympians

The men's basketball team the United States sent to play in the 2004 Summer Games in Athens, Greece, was the youngest to ever take an Olympic court since professional players were allowed to compete, starting in 1992. LeBron James was nineteen years old, and Carmelo Anthony was twenty years old. Emeka Okafor, a University of Connecticut standout, hadn't yet played in the NBA. Amar'e Stoudemire, Carlos Boozer, and Dwyane Wade altogether had just five years of professional basketball experience. Team USA Men's Basketball won a bronze medal in Athens in 2004.

In the 2008 Beijing Games, the team went undefeated and brought back the gold medal for the USA. In a 2012 match versus Australia, LeBron James tallied the first triple-double in American Olympic play since 1976: He put up eleven points, fourteen rebounds, and twelve assists. In the gold medal final match against Spain, he scored nineteen points to become Team USA men's Olympic basketball's all-time leading scorer up to that time.

LeBron James and Michael Jordan are the only players to have earned an Olympic gold medal in the same years they won NBA regular-season MVP awards, NBA Finals MVP awards, and NBA championship titles.

The Big Three had a tough time adjusting through their first professional season together, but the Heat managed to reach the championship final. In the end, they lost to the Dallas Mavericks. LeBron took the defeat hard. In the offseason, he worked on his game with Hall of Fame basketball player Hakeem Olajuwon, one of the

NBA's best centers. Improving his abilities helped LeBron find an inner calm and a renewed joy in playing basketball. It also helped him move on from the unpleasantness he'd endured since leaving Cleveland.

The superteam created by LeBron, Dwyane, and Chris ironed out its wrinkles and showed its power in its second season together. The Heat reached the championship finals again, and this time the team won by beating the Oklahoma City Thunder. LeBron finally had the championship ring he had worked so hard for and left his home in Ohio to earn.

Between LeBron's third and fourth season with the Heat, he realized he wanted another kind of ring: A wedding ring. He and Savannah were married on September 14, 2013, in San Diego,

California. Their wedding was an extravagant three-day event attended by some of the biggest names in sports, television, movies, and music.

LeBron was a happily married man in 2013 when he led the Heat to its third appearance in the NBA championship finals. The Miami Heat

beat the San Antonio Spurs to win their second NBA championship. When the Heat returned to the finals in 2014, they became the first team in twenty-seven years to reach the NBA Finals for four straight years. Unfortunately, this time the team came up short, and the Spurs won the championship.

Later that same year, LeBron's family continued to grow. His daughter, Zhuri Nova, was born on October 22, 2014. LeBron and Savannah had already had two sons, Bronny and Bryce. They were so happy to have a daughter, too.

Zhuri Nova James

LeBron and the Heat reached the NBA championship finals four times and were victorious twice, back to back. Each time the

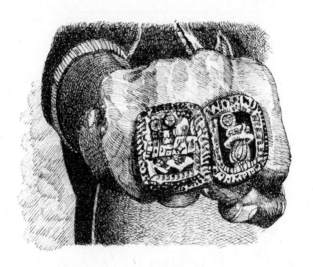

Heat won, LeBron was named the finals MVP—
Most Valuable Player. LeBron turned thirty years
old at the end of 2014. He had two championship
rings. But something bothered him: He still
hadn't won a championship for his home team of
Cleveland.

CHAPTER 7
The Chosen One Goes Home

CLEVELAND

AKRON

OHIO

In 2014, LeBron had the championship ring he had dreamed of. He had two of them. He wanted another one but not for himself and not for the Miami Heat.

LeBron had grown up in Akron, Ohio. The family he'd been born to was in Ohio. The family that had chosen him was in Ohio. The city of Cleveland had adopted him as its own when he played for the Cavaliers there. LeBron missed Ohio. And he had a new dream. He didn't want just another NBA championship ring. He wanted an NBA championship ring for Cleveland.

In a July 11, 2014, letter published in *Sports Illustrated*, LeBron announced that he was going home to Cleveland to play for the Cavaliers.

Kyrie Irving

Any bad feelings about LeBron's exit from the team seemed to be instantly forgotten. Cleveland fans were quick to forgive him. The Cavaliers made changes to improve the team and to give LeBron better support. Kyrie Irving, a very good point guard, was already on the team. The Cavs brought in Kevin Love, a talented power forward/center, from the Minnesota Timberwolves.

LeBron's first season homecoming with the Cavaliers had a bittersweet ending. The team made it to the NBA Finals, but injuries put Kyrie and

Kevin Love

Kevin on the sidelines. Without two of their most talented players, LeBron and the Cavs lost to Steph Curry and the mighty Golden State Warriors. This was the beginning of a great rivalry between LeBron and Steph.

LeBron James and Steph Curry

Stephen Curry (1988–)

Wardell Stephen "Steph" Curry II was born in Akron, Ohio. His mother, Sonya, was an educator. His father, Dell, was playing for the Cleveland Cavaliers when Steph was born.

Steph was a standout high-school basketball player at Charlotte Christian School. He played college basketball for Davidson in North Carolina. He earned many scoring and player honors. Steph decided to skip his senior year of college to enter the 2009 NBA Draft. He was selected by the Golden State Warriors. Steph has led the Warriors to three NBA championships. He has been named NBA MVP twice and an All-Star seven times.

The Cavaliers returned to the finals the following year, in 2016. Once again, LeBron and the Cavs had to face Steph Curry and the Golden State Warriors. The Cavaliers were the Eastern Conference champion. The Golden State Warriors were the Western Conference champion. The Cavs finished their regular season 57–25.

The Warriors finished with a record-breaking 73–9. For the second season in a row, Steph Curry was named NBA regular-season MVP. The Warriors had set several other records, including becoming the first team to make more than 1,000 three-pointers during the regular season. (Their total was 1,077.) The Warriors entered the finals with the better record, but would they be the better team?

LeBron was playing in his sixth straight NBA Finals. The Warriors won the first two games of the seven-game final series on their home court in Oakland, California. The teams played the next two games in Cleveland. Back on their home court, the Cavs beat the Warriors in the third game, but they lost the fourth. The teams returned to Oakland with the Warriors up three games to one against the Cavs.

It's hard to come back after losing three games in a best-of-seven championship finals series, but the Cavs refused to give up easily. LeBron and Kyrie each scored forty-one points to lead Cleveland to victory in the fifth game on the Warriors' home court. Both teams returned to Cleveland for the sixth game, where LeBron again scored forty-one points in a Cavs win that tied the series at three games each. Steph Curry fouled out of the game when he threw his mouthpiece angrily in frustration.

Game seven was played back in Oakland, where the Warriors would have the home-court advantage. No team in NBA history had ever come back from so far behind to win the championship. No team, that is, until the 2016 Cavaliers. Both teams played well and worked very hard, but when the final buzzer sounded, the Cleveland Cavaliers had beat the Golden State Warriors, 93–89. The

Cavaliers became the first team ever to win an NBA championship after trailing three games to one. Even better, the Cavs had won its very first NBA championship, and Cleveland's first pro-sports championship in fifty-two years!

LeBron had made another dream come true for himself and for the city he loved. He had returned to Cleveland to bring a championship to his beloved city, and he had done it! LeBron was named the finals MVP by unanimous vote.

With LeBron back on the freshly confident, stronger team, the Cavaliers returned to the finals in 2017 and 2018. They faced the Golden State Warriors both years. They didn't win, but LeBron became one of a few players in the NBA's history to play in eight NBA championships in a row.

CHAPTER 8
Following the Footsteps of Legends

After four seasons with the Cavaliers, in 2018, LeBron decided to change teams once again. Both he and the Cleveland Cavs had their championship rings. It was time for a new dream. LeBron signed with the Los Angeles Lakers, a team known for great players as well as great coaches. Kobe Bryant, Shaquille O'Neal, Magic Johnson, Wilt Chamberlain, and Kareem Abdul-Jabbar are just a few of the players who brought fame and championships to the Lakers. Pat Riley, Phil Jackson, and Jerry West are three of the coaches who led the team to greatness.

The Lakers had lost some of their past brilliance by the time LeBron joined the team.

Magic Johnson

LeBron believed he could help the Lakers regain their former glory. When LeBron joined the team in July 2018, he was injured. He had gotten a severe bone bruise in his right hand in May, after the Cavaliers lost the first game in the championship finals against their familiar rival, the Golden State Warriors. But LeBron still gave his best to his new team.

LeBron was injured on December 25, 2018, in a Lakers matchup versus the Warriors. The injury took LeBron out for seventeen games. He had never before had an injury that benched him for so long. For the first time in his sixteen years in the NBA, LeBron was unable to finish the regular season. It was the first time since his second season in the NBA that he missed the playoffs, breaking his personal best of thirteen straight postseasons. The year wasn't all bad for LeBron. In December 2019, he would be named the Associated Press Male Athlete of the Decade for 2008–2018. Also in 2019, in a November game versus the Oklahoma City Thunder, he became the first NBA player to post a triple-double (double-digit totals in points scored, rebounds, and assists) against all thirty teams in the league.

LeBron's second season with the Lakers came to an abrupt halt when the NBA suspended all games on March 11, 2020, after Utah Jazz center Rudy Gobert tested positive for COVID-19, a disease that was spreading quickly around the world, infecting and killing many people. When basketball resumed in July, the season was shortened. LeBron's second season with the Lakers improved, partly because Los Angeles brought superstar power forward/center Anthony Davis to the team from the New Orleans Pelicans. The now-healthy LeBron and Anthony complemented

LeBron James and Anthony Davis

each other wonderfully. The Lakers earned their way into the playoffs with the best record in the Western Conference in the shortened regular season.

The Lakers beat LeBron's former team, the Miami Heat, to win its seventeenth NBA title. Together, LeBron and Anthony averaged 54.8

points per game in the finals. LeBron was the top scorer for the Lakers in the postseason, and Anthony was second. Shaquille O'Neal and Kobe Bryant were the last Lakers duo to have been the top two postseason scorers (2004). LeBron won another NBA Finals MVP—his fourth in four championship wins.

The Lakers win the 2020 NBA Championship.

LeBron's third Lakers season began in December 2020, only a few months after the end of the COVID-shortened previous season. This didn't give the Lakers or the Heat much time to rest between seasons. And the lack of rest time affected the Lakers. LeBron sprained his ankle, Anthony Davis strained a calf muscle, and Dennis Schröder had to quarantine away from the team after being exposed to the virus. The loss of such strong players hurt the team, but the Lakers still made it to the playoffs. Unfortunately, Los Angeles lost in the first round of the postseason to the Phoenix Suns.

CHAPTER 9
Striving for Greatness in All Things

As much as LeBron has done on the court, he has been just as active off it.

The LeBron James Family Foundation was the first jewel in LRMR Ventures, LeBron's businesses outside of basketball. LRMR stands for LeBron, Rich, Maverick, and Randy, the names of LeBron and his three business partners: Rich Paul, Maverick Carter, and Randy Mims, LeBron's childhood friends. LeBron is also part owner of the English Premier League football (soccer) team Liverpool as well as part owner of the Boston Red Sox baseball team. Pizza is one of LeBron's favorite foods, and he is a founder of the Blaze Pizza stores.

LeBron's popularity makes him well liked by

companies who want him to represent them and
their products. Nike was the first company to hire
LeBron to endorse them, before he even joined
the NBA. LeBron has named some of the Nike
athletic shoes that carry his name after places
that were important to him growing up. Dunkin'
Donuts, Walmart, GMC, and Upper Deck are
just a few of the other companies proud to be
represented by LeBron.

Few athletes are as dedicated to helping people as LeBron. From the LeBron James Family Foundation came the creation of the I Promise program. LeBron knows very few can change their lives through professional sports. He believes anyone can transform their life through education. The I Promise program began in 2015 by providing academic support and other resources for struggling students in LeBron's hometown of Akron. In partnership with the University of Akron, LeBron enabled students to work toward earning full college scholarships. A year later, the I Promise Institute was established on the University of Akron campus. The Institute gives students a chance to become accustomed to college life.

One of the most important things LeBron has ever created is the I Promise School, which opened its doors to 240 third- and fourth-grade students on July 30, 2018. The school is dedicated to making sure that students have every resource they need for academic and personal success. I Promise Village was opened in 2020. It's a place where students facing problems such as homelessness can go to find housing and other forms of assistance.

In 2020, Kent State University in Ohio joined the I Promise family by agreeing to offer free tuition to I Promise students. And in August of that year, LeBron published his first children's book, which became an instant bestseller. It is called *I Promise*. The book was inspired by his foundation's promise to motivate young people to strive for greatness.

Along with education, LeBron has interests in entertainment, including television and movies. Springhill Entertainment is one of the companies LeBron created with Maverick Carter. Springhill produced a television miniseries titled *I Promise*, which tells the story of the I Promise program.

LeBron opens the I Promise School

LeBron uses his fame to bring attention to social problems. In 2012, LeBron and his Miami Heat teammates wore hoodies before a game to bring attention to the death of Trayvon Martin, a Black teenager who was killed by a member of a neighborhood watch group. When Eric Garner, a Black man, was killed by a New York City policeman in 2014, LeBron and the rest of the Cleveland Cavaliers players wore "I Can't Breathe" T-shirts before a game.

In 2018, when LeBron spoke about politics during an interview with ESPN about his experience as a Black man in America, talk show host Laura Ingraham said LeBron should keep his opinions to himself and "shut up and dribble." LeBron knows he owes more than dribbling to his fans and community, and he's earned the right to use his voice. "The best thing she did was help me create more awareness," LeBron said in response. "We will definitely not shut up and dribble . . . I mean too much to society, too much to the youth, too much to so many kids who feel like they don't have a way out."

LeBron dealt with Ingraham's insult in a unique way. He produced a cable television show titled *Shut Up and Dribble*. The show is a three-part documentary about the role of Black American athletes in culture and politics.

On August 26, 2020, LeBron and every team

in the NBA refused to play in protest of the shooting of a young Black man named Jacob Blake in Kenosha, Wisconsin. LeBron has spoken out against many incidences of racial and social injustice, even when it meant angering or losing fans. He also helped form an organization called More Than a Vote, which encourages people of color to vote and fights efforts to make voting more difficult for them.

LeBron is inspired by athletic greats of the past, such as former Lakers star Kareem Abdul-Jabbar, former football player Jim Brown, and boxing champion Muhammad Ali. "[These are guys who stood up] when it was way worse than it is today," LeBron said of the athletes who inspire his activism. "Hopefully, someday down the line, people will recognize me not only for the way I approached the game of basketball, but the way I approached life as an African American man."

Playing basketball isn't the only way LeBron entertains people. He's also an actor. In 2021, he starred in *Space Jam: A New Legacy*, along with Zendaya and Michael B. Jordan. The movie was a sequel to the original *Space Jam* starring basketball superstar Michael Jordan in 1996. LeBron and his friend Maverick helped produce the movie.

Basketball, his businesses, and activism are important to LeBron, but his most important role

is being a dad and husband. Bronny, Bryce, and Zhuri are the joy of LeBron's life, and he refers to his wife, Savannah, as his queen.

LeBron never forgot the pain of growing up without a father or his mother's struggles as a single parent. He never forgot the example of fatherhood set by Frank Walker Sr. Even with his busy playing schedule and various businesses, LeBron is a loving father who takes an active interest in his children's lives.

LeBron continues to maintain a very high level of play. On February 7, 2023, he scored thirty-eight points against the Oklahoma City Thunder, breaking Kareem Abdul-Jabbar's thirty-eight-year-old NBA career scoring record of 38,387 points, making him arguably the greatest NBA player of all time.

As NBA Commissioner Adam Silver has said about LeBron, "His basketball history is still being written."

LeBron James Career Highlights

NBA's top scoring champion (2023)

Four NBA Championships (2012, 2013, 2016, 2020)

Four NBA MVP Awards (2009, 2010, 2012, 2013)

Four NBA Finals MVP Awards (2012, 2013, 2016, 2020)

Three-Time Olympic Medalist (Bronze 2004, Gold 2008, Gold 2012)

Seventeen NBA All-Star Games (2005–2021)

NBA Rookie of the Year (2003–2004)

Three-Time *Sports Illustrated* Sportsperson of the Year (2012, 2016, 2020)

Seven-Time Best NBA Player ESPY Award (2007, 2009, 2012, 2013, 2016, 2017, 2018)

Three-Time Best Male Athlete ESPY Award (2012, 2013, 2016)

Three-Time Associated Press Athlete of the Year (2013, 2016, 2018)

Associated Press Male Athlete of the Decade (2010s)

Timeline of LeBron James's Life

1984	LeBron Raymone James born in Akron, Ohio, December 30
1994	Moves in with Coach Frank Walker Sr.'s family
2002	Dubbed "The Chosen One" by *Sports Illustrated* magazine
2003	Chosen first by the Cleveland Cavaliers in the NBA Draft
2004	Becomes NBA Rookie of the Year
2009	Named NBA MVP for first time
2010	Joins Miami Heat
2012	Wins first NBA Championship
2013	Becomes youngest player to score twenty thousand points in the NBA
	Wins second NBA Championship with Miami Heat
	Marries Savannah Brinson on September 14
2014	Returns to the Cleveland Cavaliers
2016	Leads Cleveland to its first-ever NBA Championship, LeBron's third
2018	Joins the Los Angeles Lakers
2020	Leads Lakers to NBA Championship, LeBron's fourth
2023	Scores thirty-eight points against the Oklahoma City Thunder to become NBA's all-time scoring leader

Timeline of the World

1984 — The movie *Ghostbusters* premieres on June 7

1987 — Teddy Seymour becomes the first Black man to sail solo around the world

1994 — Nelson Mandela elected president of South Africa in the country's first interracial election

1998 — Google Inc. is founded in Menlo Park, California, by Larry Page and Sergey Brin

2001 — Terrorists hijack jetliners and fly them into the World Trade Center, the Pentagon, and a Pennsylvania field

2003 — Apple launches iTunes, selling one million songs in its first week

2004 — Boston Red Sox win the Major League Baseball World Series for first time since 1918

2009 — Barack Obama sworn in as the forty-fourth president of the United States

2010 — Instagram is founded by Kevin Systrom

2014 — Michael Sam becomes the first openly gay NFL draft pick

2018 — Prince Harry, the Duke of Sussex, marries American actor Meghan Markle

2020 — Los Angeles Lakers basketball legend Kobe Bryant and his daughter Gianna Bryant are killed in a helicopter accident

Bibliography

*Books for young readers

*Bryant, Howard. *Legends: The Best Players, Games, and Teams in Basketball*. New York: Philomel Books, 2017.

*Christopher, Matt. *On the Court with . . . LeBron James*. Matt Christopher Sports Bio Bookshelf. New York: Little, Brown and Company, 2008.

Geoffreys, Clayton. *LeBron James: The Inspiring Story of One of Basketball's Greatest Players*. Basketball Biography Books. Winter Park, FL: Calvintir Books, LLC, 2020.

*James, LeBron, with Buzz Bissinger. *LeBron's Dream Team: How Four Friends and I Brought a Championship Home*. New York: Penguin Books, 2009.

Windhorst, Brian, and Dave McMenamin. *Return of the King: LeBron James, the Cleveland Cavaliers, and the Greatest Comeback in NBA History*. New York: Grand Central Publishing, 2017.

*Zuckerman, Gregory, with Elijah and Gabriel Zuckerman. *Rising Above: How 11 Athletes Overcame Challenges in Their Youth to Become Stars*. New York: Philomel Books, 2016.